Masters of Music

THE WORLD'S GREATEST COMPOSERS

The Life and Times of

Peter Ilyich Tchaikovsky

Mitchell Lane
PUBLISHERS

P.O. Box 196
Hockessin, Delaware 19707

Masters of Music

THE WORLD'S GREATEST COMPOSERS

Titles in the Series

The Life and Times of...

Visit us on the web: www.mitchelllane.com
Comments? email us: mitchelllane@mitchelllane.com

Masters of Music
THE WORLD'S GREATEST COMPOSERS

The Life and Times of

Peter Ilyich Tchaikovsky

by Jim Whiting

Printing   2   3   4   5   6   7   8

    Library of Congress Cataloging-in-Publication Data
Whiting, Jim, 1943-
        The life and times of Peter Ilyich Tchaikovsky/Jim Whiting.
              p. cm. — (Masters of Music. The world's greatest composers)
    Summary: Chronicles the troubled life of the nineteenth-century Russian composer.
Includes sidebars on such topics as serfs, Leo Tolstoy, and the invention of the phono-
graph.
    Includes bibliographical references (p.) and index.
        ISBN 1-58415-211-7 (lib bdg.)
        1. Tchaikovsky, Peter Ilyich, 1840-1893—Juvenile literature. 2. Composers—Russia—
Biography—Juvenile literature. [1. Tchaikovsky, Peter Ilyich, 1840-1893. 2. Composers.] I.
Title. II. Series.
ML3930.C4W53 2003
780'.92—dc21   2003000354

TCHAIKOVSKY, P.
C.1

ABOUT THE AUTHOR: Jim Whiting has been a journalist, writer, editor, and photographer for more than 20 years. In addition to a lengthy stint as publisher of *Northwest Runner* magazine, Mr. Whiting has contributed articles to the *Seattle Times*, *Conde Nast Traveler*, *Newsday*, and *Saturday Evening Post*. He has edited more than 60 titles in the Mitchell Lane Real-Life Reader Biography series and Unlocking the Secrets of Science. He is the author of numerous books for young adults, including *Charles Schulz* and *The Life and Times of Johann Sebastian Bach* (Mitchell Lane). His love of classical music inspired him to write this book. He lives in Washington state with his wife and two teenage sons.

PUBLISHER'S NOTE: This story is based on the author's extensive research, which he believes to be accurate. Documentation of such research is contained on page 46.

The internet sites referenced herein were active as of the publication date. Due to the fleeting nature of some Web sites, we cannot guarantee they will all be active when you are reading this book.

Contents

The Life and Times of
Peter Ilyich Tchaikovsky

by Jim Whiting

* For Your Information

The opening Christmas party scene in Tchaikovsky's ballet The Nutcracker.
Herr Drosselmeier, in the center, is the somewhat mysterious godfather of
Clara, the ballet's heroine. Here, he is providing entertainment for the party
guests with two life-sized mechanical dolls he has built in his workshop.

CHAPTER I

A Happy Dance, An Unhappy Man

The Christmas holiday season wouldn't be complete for many families without attending a performance of *The Nutcracker* ballet. It is probably the world's most popular ballet because it appeals to people of all ages. Children as young as three and four romp about the theater lobby before the show. The little girls are often wearing new dresses, while the boys may be wearing freshly ironed shirts and ties for the first time. Everyone is ready to have a good time.

When the audience has settled in their seats, the overhead lights grow dim. Soon the auditorium is almost entirely dark. Then the conductor comes out, raises his baton, and the bright and bubbly overture begins. The overture sets the mood for the rest of the show.

The festive feeling continues as the curtain rises on the annual Christmas party hosted by the Stahlbaum family. There is a beautiful Christmas tree and everyone is enjoying themselves, especially the two Stahlbaum children, Clara and Fritz. Many of their friends are there.

Then Herr Drosselmeier makes an appearance. He is the godfather of both Clara and Fritz and has presents for them. Clara's gift is a large nutcracker doll. Fritz is jealous; he snatches it away and damages it. Though Clara is heartbroken, Drosselmeier manages to repair it. Not long afterward, the party comes to an end. The guests leave, and the Stahlbaums go upstairs to get ready for bed. But Clara is worried about her new toy and can't sleep. So she goes back downstairs to check on it.

Then something magical happens. The Christmas tree grows much larger, and some mice, under the leadership of the gigantic Mouse King, come running onto the stage. The Nutcracker comes to life and calls for help. Many toy soldiers respond, and there is a big battle. The mice are winning and the Mouse King is about to stab the Nutcracker with a sword. Just before that can happen, Clara throws her shoe at the Mouse King. It strikes him on the head and he collapses. The rest of the mice retreat.

The Nutcracker thanks Clara and turns into a handsome prince. He leads her through an enchanted forest with many dancing snowflakes. Then they take a long voyage to his kingdom. His subjects are happy to see him, and they perform several dances in Clara's honor. The entertainment reaches its peak with the famous Waltz of the Flowers and the Dance of the Sugar Plum Fairy. When the dancing finally ends, Clara and the prince prepare to leave. Everyone in the kingdom waves good-bye.

A few moments later, Clara wakes up. She is back in her house. It has all been a dream. And what a dream!—with dancers in elaborate, beautiful costumes, swirling about the stage in almost constant colorful movement, and set decorations all brilliantly painted.

But the most memorable part of *The Nutcracker* is the uplifting music. The tunes are all bright and cheerful. Even people who don't

Another scene from The Nutcracker. *A few minutes after showing off his mechanical dolls, Herr Drosselmeier presents Clara with her gift, a toy nutcracker. All the children want to touch it. Later both the toy and the Christmas tree in the background become much larger.*

listen to classical music have probably heard parts of *The Nutcracker* in advertisements, as background music while they do their Christmas shopping, or at other times when someone is trying to create an upbeat atmosphere.

It is only natural to assume that *The Nutcracker*'s composer was a bright and cheerful man. After all, how could anyone who wasn't happy write such glad music?

In reality, the composer was actually very depressed as he was writing *The Nutcracker*. He had been depressed for much of his life, but things had been getting worse. His beloved sister had just died. One of his most cherished friends had recently abandoned him.

After its premiere in 1892, *The Nutcracker* was publicly criticized. The composer himself would be dead within a year.

His name was Peter Ilyich Tchaikovsky.

"The Waltz of the Snowflakes" from The Nutcracker. *This scene comes at the end of Act I after Clara and the Prince have defeated the Mouse King.*

Napoléon Invades Russia

In early 1812, emperor Napoléon Bonaparte of France controlled nearly all of Europe. He decided to force Russia, under Czar Alexander I, to submit to him as well. Napoléon gathered what he called his Grand Armée, a force of about half a million men. It was almost certainly the largest army ever assembled. At the beginning of the summer, in June, he led his troops into Russia.

The Russians were commanded by Field Marshal Mikhail Kutuzov. He knew that he didn't have enough men to stand up to Napoléon in a direct battle, but he had a plan. As Napoléon advanced deeper into Russia, he ordered his men to destroy the crops so that Napoléon couldn't use Russian food to feed his army.

Eventually Napoléon's forces began to decline. He lost some men to sickness and hunger. Others deserted. Still more were lost in battle. Within three months, two-thirds of his troops were gone. But it was clear that he still had enough soldiers to capture Moscow, Russia's largest city.

To protect Moscow, Alexander ordered Kutuzov to fight Napoléon in a pitched battle. The two armies met on September 7 at Borodino, a town about seventy miles west of Moscow. Napoléon sent wave after wave of soldiers against entrenched Russians. Both sides lost thousands of men. By the time the fighting stopped in the late afternoon, neither side had won a definite victory. Kutuzov withdrew.

Napoléon entered the city a week later to find it almost deserted. Soon afterward, a huge fire burned down most of the buildings. That meant that there would be no shelter for the French army during the upcoming winter. Finally, Napoléon began heading back to the warmer parts of Europe. But he had waited too long.

Russian winters are famous for their severity, and the winter of 1812 was one of the worst on record. Snow began to fall soon after Napoléon left Moscow. The temperatures were often below zero. There was almost no food. Small bands of Russians, who were familiar with the land, continually attacked the exhausted and starving French. In early December, Napoléon abandoned what was left of his army and rode in a carriage back to France. Only about 10,000 of his troops survived. It was a devastating defeat.

Tchaikovsky wrote the *1812 Overture* in 1880 to commemorate the Russian victory. Today, it is one of his most popular compositions. In many live performances, cannons and old-time rifles are used in addition to standard orchestral instruments.

A picture of Peter Tchaikovsky taken while he was a student at the School for Jurisprudence. Tchaikovsky spent several years training to become a lawyer. In his spare time, he played the piano. Though he worked for the government for a few years, he didn't enjoy his job. Eventually he gave it up and became a full-time music student.

A Sensitive Boy

Peter Ilyich Tchaikovsky was born on May 7, 1840. He was the second child of Alexandra and Ilya Petrovich Tchaikovsky. Peter's father had been married once before, but his wife had died within two years. He remarried in 1833, when he was thirty and his new wife was twenty.

The couple's first child, a boy, Nikolay, was born in 1838. Within twelve years there would be a total of six children: Nikolay and Peter; a girl, Alexandra; and three more boys, Ippolit and twins Modest and Anatol. They all had a half sister, Zinaida, the only child from their father's first marriage.

When Peter was born, the family lived on a small estate in Votkinsk, a town near the Ural Mountains in central Russia. The estate included a few serfs, or peasants. His father was an important man, employed as the manager of the Kamsko-Votkinsk Iron Mines. His mother was a cultured woman whose father was French and mother was Russian. She played the piano during social gatherings at the family's home. Young Peter was quick to imitate her.

When Peter was four, his mother hired a governess, a young French woman named Fanny Durbach. Because of the

Tchaikovskys' social position, the children's mother didn't want to send the children to the local schools. Fanny's main responsibility was to take care of Nikolay and their cousin Lydia, who lived with the family, and provide them with an education. But the governess quickly made young Peter her favorite.

From an early age, Peter was a very sensitive boy. Fanny described him as a "child of porcelain." Because of his delicate nature, she explained, "I had to be very careful how I treated him. With him there would be no question of punishment: the least criticism or reproof of a kind that would pass lightly over other children would upset him alarmingly."

As is sometimes the case with sensitive, shy boys, he became very devoted to his mother. For some reason, he was especially attracted to her hands.

"Such hands do not exist nowadays, and never will again," he wrote much later in his life.

Despite his extreme sensitivity, the youngster was like many other children in one respect: He didn't pay much attention to neatness. His clothes "were always in disorder," Fanny recalled much later. "Either he had stained them in his absent-mindedness, or buttons were missing, or his hair was only half-brushed."

While his older brother was a slow learner, Peter was a bright boy who quickly absorbed what Fanny was teaching them. He spoke French and German by the time he was six. But there was one area where he disagreed with Fanny. When the lessons were finished, she wanted him to spend his time outdoors.

Peter often crossed her. He enjoyed playing the piano. The house also had a huge device known as an orchestrion. It was similar to a barrel organ and contained a number of pipes of different lengths that made sounds similar to the various instruments of an orchestra. Young Peter loved to sit beside it for hours on end, listening to selections from operas and other music. German composer Wolfgang Amadeus Mozart was his favorite, and many times during his later life he said that Mozart had been a major influence on the way that he wrote music.

Often he would listen to a piece of music on the orchestrion, then rush over to the piano and try to play what he had just heard. Soon the family hired a piano tutor, a young woman who was a freed serf. Peter quickly progressed beyond the limited lessons that she could provide.

What must have been a happy existence came to an abrupt end in 1848, when Peter was eight. His mother was unhappy living in the country and wanted to live somewhere with a more active social scene. So his father resigned his position in Votkinsk and accepted another job in Moscow, Russia's largest city. Fanny was released from her position with the family and left without saying good-bye to Peter. Peter would not see her again for forty-four years.

When the Tchaikovskys arrived in Moscow, they learned that a so-called family friend had snatched the job away. In addition, an epidemic of cholera was raging in the city. The family decided to keep going and wound up in St. Petersburg, the nation's capital. When Peter and Nikolay began school there, their classmates made fun of them. They laughed and called them "country bumpkins." Both boys came down with measles. Nikolay made a normal recovery. The more sensitive Peter, who had always been subject to nervous illnesses, was ordered to bed for several months.

To add to the confusion, his father finally found a job with another mining company, but it was located hundreds of miles away, near the Siberian border. Nikolay remained behind at a school in St. Petersburg. With both his brother and Fanny gone, Peter must have felt very alone.

Then, in 1850, his parents decided to send him to another school in St. Petersburg. It was called the School of Jurisprudence, and it would eventually educate its students for careers in law. Peter would become a student in the school's preparatory department.

Because the family lived so far away, Peter would have to be a boarding student—he would have to live at the school. Modest Vakar, a family friend, agreed to act as the boy's guardian during his time there. Peter's mother made the long trip with Peter to help him settle in to his new life.

A scene from Moscow in the nineteenth century. The large building on the left with the unusual shaped domes is part of the Kremlin. It was the official residence of the czars. The bell tower on the right is nearly 300 feet high.

Just before she was ready to leave, as a parting treat she took him to an opera by Mikhail Glinka, who is considered the father of Russian music. It made a great impression on the youngster.

But soon afterward came the moment for her departure.

Peter completely lost his self-control. He clung desperately to his mother and screamed at the top of his voice for her not to go. He had to be pulled away from her so that she could get into her carriage. As the carriage began to pull away, Peter broke free and ran after it and even managed to grab it. As the vehicle began to pick up speed, he lost his grip and fell off onto the street.

A street scene in St. Petersburg. The city was founded in 1703 by Czar Peter the Great on 44 islands in the delta of the Neva River. For more than two centuries, it was the capital of Russia. Today it is the country's second-largest city and a popular tourist destination.

"To his life's end Tchaikovsky could never recall this hour without a shiver of horror," wrote his younger brother Modest, who would become Peter's closest confidant in later life.

Making matters worse, a scarlet fever epidemic raged through the school not long after Peter's arrival. Modest Vakar brought Peter to stay with his family until it subsided. Vakar's own son soon caught the disease and died. Though the Vakars assured Peter that he wasn't responsible, he still blamed himself for the tragedy. This tendency to take the blame for things that he wasn't personally responsible for would have a great effect later in his life.

When the epidemic died down, Peter returned to school. Somehow he managed to adjust to life on his own and did well in school. But he didn't see his family for nearly two years and was almost always homesick.

He got some good news when his father retired in 1852. The Tchaikovskys moved to St. Petersburg and Peter was reunited with his family. He did very well on the entrance examinations for the School of Jurisprudence and began studying there in the fall. Though his classes took up most of his time, there was a little left over to study and play music.

For more than a year and a half, Peter enjoyed peace and happiness. Then a horrible event happened in the summer of 1854.

His mother died of cholera. ◈

THE SERFS

The Civil War, which began in 1861, was ultimately responsible for freeing the slaves in the United States. In Russia, 1861 was also the year in which the serfs, or peasants, were set free. For several centuries, they had lived under conditions that closely resembled those of slaves.

For much of Russia's history it was relatively easy for peasants to move from place to place. But starting with Czar Ivan IV—who ruled from 1533 to 1584 and was known as Ivan the Terrible—restrictions were placed on their freedom of movement.

Beginning with Ivan, the czars began taking political power away from the major landholding nobles. In return, they gave the nobles more power to run their estates. Many of these estates were huge and required a dependable source of manpower. The serfs became legally bound to the noble who owned the estate where they worked. In addition, serfdom became hereditary. If you were born a serf, you almost certainly remained a serf for the rest of your life, as would your children.

This system of serfdom continued for several hundred years. It is somewhat ironic that if Napoléon had succeeded in his Russian invasion in 1812, the serfs would probably have been freed at that time. But he failed, and the system continued for nearly fifty more years.

When Russia lost the Crimean War in 1856 to the combined armies of Britain, France, and Turkey, it became obvious that the country had to modernize in order to keep up with the more industrialized countries of Western Europe. Czar Alexander II began laying plans to free the serfs. Many of the Russian nobles objected. They depended on having hundreds or thousands of serfs to work their huge landholdings.

But Alexander remained firm. "It is better to abolish serfdom from above than to wait for the time when it will begin to abolish itself from below," he said. He issued the Emancipation Manifesto in 1861, which ordered the immediate freeing of the serfs. From then on, they could buy their own land. Their movement could no longer be restricted.

Many continued to live in poverty, however—especially since their former masters often took advantage of them. Most serfs were poorly educated and didn't fully understand their new rights. Land prices were often very high. It wasn't until the Russian Revolution of 1917 and the abolition of private property that serfdom finally came to an end.

This is a picture of Anton Rubinstein, who played an important role in Tchaikovsky's development. He was one of Europe's greatest pianists and composed 20 operas, six symphonies and a great deal of other music. He established the St. Petersburg Conservatory, where he became Tchaikovsky's composition teacher. Soon afterward, Anton's brother Nikolay established the Moscow Conservatory. Nikolay provided Tchaikovsky with additional encouragement.

CHAPTER

3

A Musical Career Begins

Tchaikovsky may have never completely recovered from his mother's death. Twenty-five years later he wrote, "Every moment of that appalling day is as vivid to me as though it was yesterday."

The tragedy may be the reason that much of his music was about doomed women: Juliet in *Romeo and Juliet;* Joan of Arc; Odette in his ballet *Swan Lake*, a woman cursed by a wizard and changed into a swan; Francesca da Rimini, a beautiful young woman forced into a loveless marriage who falls in love with another man and is murdered; and Tatyana in *Eugene Onegin,* his most famous opera, who falls in love with someone who deceives her.

But even without his mother, life had to go on. Tchaikovsky continued to do well at school. He attended many musical performances. Somehow he found the time to study piano and singing. Sometimes he even thought about becoming a musician instead of a lawyer.

But one of his piano teachers wasn't very impressed. He wrote to Peter's father, advising against letting his son pursue a career in music.

"In the first place, I saw no signs of genius in Tchaikovsky, and secondly because in my experience the lot of a musician in Russia at that time was an onerous one," the teacher said.

He was half wrong, half right.

He admitted to being wrong after Tchaikovsky became famous. "I must admit, to my great embarrassment, that at no time did it occur to me that Tchaikovsky had in him the stuff of a musician," he said.

But he was right about "the lot of a musician." Russia didn't have the same respectful attitude toward musicians that many countries in Western Europe did. Even geniuses such as Beethoven and Mozart would have had a hard time earning a living if they had been Russians.

Tchaikovsky's growing enthusiasm about music may have been the main reason he gradually started losing interest in his legal studies. When he graduated from the School of Jurisprudence in 1859, he was ranked in the lower half of his class. Despite this low ranking, however, he got a job as a clerk at the Ministry of Justice in St. Petersburg. For two years, his life was very routine. He went to work in the morning, spent all day on the job, then went to the theater, opera, or other musical performance in the evening. He had developed into a handsome young man and was popular at house parties because of his ability to play the piano.

Then, in 1861, for reasons that no one has ever determined, his father encouraged him to study music. For a young man who was always plagued with self-doubt, this sudden approval by his father gave him the confidence he needed. And the timing was nearly perfect.

The Russian Musical Society had been formed less than two years earlier. Its founders wanted to raise the country's musical standards. Soon the organization gained its most important backer: Czar Alexander II himself. In 1862 the society opened a conservatory in St. Petersburg. It was housed in a large building, which provided ample space where music classes could be taught.

Tchaikovsky was one of its first students, enrolling part-time.

Two days after beginning his studies, he wrote to his sister: "I have come to the conclusion that sooner or later I shall give up my present occupation for music." During most of his legal studies, he hadn't been much of a student. That quickly changed. He had finally found something he loved and at which he was very good. Meanwhile he continued to work at the Ministry.

The "sooner or later" he mentioned to his sister happened late in 1863. He was passed over for promotion. He quickly resigned from his job and devoted himself entirely to his musical studies.

His brother Nikolay was horrified. A successful government official himself, he criticized his younger brother for entering such an "undignified profession."

Showing somewhat uncharacteristic self-confidence, Tchaikovsky replied, "The day will come when you will be proud of me."

One reason for his confidence was that Ilya Tchaikovsky continued to support his son's decision. However, with only a small retirement pension and growing children still to support, he couldn't offer much in the way of financial help. Peter added a little more money to his income by giving piano lessons.

He couldn't have been happier.

Modest remembered, "At no time in his life was [he] so cheerful and serene. In a small room which held only a bed and a writing table, he started bravely on his new and laborious existence."

Tchaikovsky was also fortunate. The director of the conservatory, Anton Rubinstein, who was also a prolific composer, took a personal interest in him. That helped Tchaikovsky to develop his skills more quickly.

He graduated from the conservatory early in 1866. One of his final requirements was to write a piece of music. It was severely criticized.

Only one man, a teacher named Herman Laroche, saw any good in it.

"I tell you frankly that I consider yours is the greatest musical talent to which Russia can look forward in the future," he wrote Tchaikovsky. "I see in you the greatest, or rather the only, hope for our musical future."

Subsequent events would prove him to be absolutely correct.

But that future fame was far away as the young man, now twenty-six, departed for Moscow. Anton Rubinstein's brother Nikolay had just opened a conservatory there. Nikolay needed a harmony teacher and Anton recommended Tchaikovsky. Nikolay became a friend as well as an employer. He let Tchaikovsky live with him for six years and treated him with a great deal of kindness.

In addition to his teaching duties, Tchaikovsky continued to compose. His Symphony #1, also called "Winter Dreams," made its debut in 1868. Later that year he conducted some of his works in public for the first time. But he had an unusual habit. Afraid that his head would literally fall off, he held on to it tightly. Not surprisingly, he wasn't a very good conductor. It would be at least ten years before he would try it again.

He also had an unsuccessful love affair that began in the fall of that year. He met a young Belgian singer named Desirée Artot. He composed a piano piece, "Romance in F," which he dedicated to her. Nevertheless, she married someone else a few months later. Tchaikovsky was very disappointed, but he snapped out of it fairly quickly.

One reason may have been that his first opera, *Voyevoda* ("Dream on the Volga"), was presented soon afterward. The audience liked it a great deal. So did music critics, with one exception: the same Herman Laroche who had praised him a few years earlier. Once again, Laroche proved to be correct: *Voyevoda* was only performed three more times, and people soon lost interest in it.

Despite this disappointment, Tchaikovsky kept on composing. He also spent large amounts of time visiting his sister, who had married by this time, and her family. He began to travel. Even

An opera singer named Desirée Artot. Tchaikovsky met her in the fall of 1868 and quickly fell in love. He even announced his engagement to her. But she soon married another singer.

though he wasn't making much money, his career continued to advance.

His Symphony #2, which is nicknamed "The Little Russian," premiered in 1873. Another opera, *The Oprichnik* ("The Life Guardsman"), made its debut the following year and was more successful than the first one.

He wrote the Piano Concerto #1 in 1875. He originally dedicated it to Nikolay Rubinstein, an excellent pianist. But Rubinstein criticized it harshly. He said that it was "unplayable." So Tchaikovsky rededicated it to the conductor Hans von Bülow, who gave the work its world premiere. Rubinstein's judgment proved to be wrong. The Piano Concerto #1 has become one of Tchaikovsky's most famous and most frequently played compositions.

The year 1876 began with the premier of his Symphony #3, continued with his completion of the famous ballet *Swan Lake,* and concluded with his face-to-face meeting with Leo Tolstoy, Russia's most famous writer.

The following year would be the most momentous of his entire life. ◆

LEO
TOLSTOY

Many people consider Leo Tolstoy to be the greatest writer who ever lived. Tolstoy was born in 1828, twelve years before Tchaikovsky. His parents owned a huge estate in Russia called Yasnaya Polyana, and the boy's first years were very privileged. But his mother died when he was only two. His grandmother and father both died when the boy was nine, and he was sent to live with relatives.

He began university studies at the age of fifteen, but he wasn't a serious student and left four years later. He traveled to Moscow, where he lived a wild life for several years.

Then he joined his brother in the army. He was involved in the Crimean War, which Russia fought against Great Britain, France, and Turkey. At this time he also began his writing career with three short novels—*Childhood*, *Boyhood,* and *Youth*—that used many of the experiences of his younger days. The novels made him famous.

In 1862 he married Sophia Behrs. Eventually he would have thirteen children with her. Soon after the wedding, he began writing what would become his best-known novel, *War and Peace*. It is about five aristocratic families in the early 1800s and includes nearly 600 different characters. It is more than 1,000 pages long. He followed this with another lengthy novel, *Anna Karenina*. The two books made him famous. They also made him very wealthy.

In later life Tolstoy became more concerned with the way that he lived. He accepted two major ideas: love for all people and nonviolent resistance against the forces of evil. For many years he wrote essays and stories about his beliefs. Eventually he wanted to give away everything he owned and live a simple life, like the peasants. His wife and most of his children were opposed to the idea.

In November 1910 he literally ran away from home. A few days later he became ill with pneumonia and stumbled into a tiny railroad station. He died soon afterward. It was a national day of mourning in Russia.

Tchaikovsky idolized Tolstoy. In 1876 Tolstoy was at the height of his fame. When he visited Moscow that December, a musical evening was held in his honor. One of Tchaikovsky's compositions was included, and Tchaikovsky sat next to Tolstoy while it was being played. Afterward, Tchaikovsky wrote, "Never in the whole course of my life did I feel so flattered, never so proud of my creative power, as when Leo Tolstoy, sitting by my side, listened to my *andante* while the tears streamed down his face."

In this scene from Tchaikovsky's ballet Swan Lake, the jester performs a solo dance. Though Swan Lake is probably the world's most popular ballet today, it was a failure when it premiered in 1877. With new choreography (the way the dancers perform) in 1895, it became successful.

CHAPTER 4

Two Women

I n March 1877, *Swan Lake* was performed for the first time. Today it is regarded by many people as the greatest ballet ever written. In 1877, it was a total flop.

But the disappointment of that failure would soon be overshadowed by Tchaikovsky's relationships with two very different women.

One of them was named Nadezhda von Meck. She was extremely wealthy and newly widowed. She felt lonely in her large house, so she tried to fill it with music. Music became her main emotional outlet.

She soon heard about Tchaikovsky and found that she liked his music. She also knew that despite his growing success, he had very little money. Early in 1877, she asked him to compose a simple piano and violin arrangement. She paid him a great deal of money when it was finished. Quickly she asked for another composition. And another. And another. Each time she paid more money. She also began writing him long letters, in which she poured out her heart and soul to him. Because this was an era before the telephone, Tchaikovsky was also used to writing long letters. He responded in kind.

Nadezhda von Meck was very influential in Tchaikovsky's life. She was a wealthy Russian widow who loved music. After hearing Tchaikovsky's music, she made an unusual bargain with him. She would support him financially, but there was one condition. They could never meet face-to-face. They occasionally passed each other on the street, but didn't say anything.

Theirs is one of the music world's most famous series of letters. Each wrote to the other hundreds of times. Since both of them saved all the letters they received, we have an accurate record of how they felt. Even though she was nine years older than he was, she appeared to have a case of hero worship. She made him an extraordinary offer. She would support him financially, but on one condition: They could never meet face-to-face. All their communications must be by letter.

They did see each other a few times in future years, but it was always by accident. They would take care not to speak. Then they would go home and write a letter about how the other one looked and send it off.

This was certainly an unusual arrangement, but it was a wonderful opportunity for Tchaikovsky. Now he was free to do what he loved—to write music—and he no longer had to worry about making a living. He may have felt that he was the luckiest man on earth.

It was a feeling that would last only a few weeks.

In May, Tchaikovsky got a letter from a former student of his. Twenty-eight-year-old Antonia Milyukova claimed that she was in love with him and adored his music. Tchaikovsky was a handsome man, and Antonia wasn't the only student who had developed a crush on him while he was teaching there.

Tchaikovsky wrote back that he didn't feel the same way. With most normal people, that would be the end. But there was very little that was normal about Antonia Milyukova.

When Tchaikovsky, not unreasonably, said that he wasn't interested in marrying her, she got very angry. She said that she would commit suicide.

Tchaikovsky's response was also not normal. Just as he had done when the Vakar boy died of scarlet fever, Tchaikovsky blamed himself for what happened. He apparently believed that somehow he had led her on, and he agreed to marry her. He tried to be honest. He said that he didn't love her. The best he could offer was his friendship. Though we might think that "just friendship" is an odd reason for marrying someone, Antonia didn't. She quickly accepted his proposal.

The marriage took place in mid-July. Their wedding picture gives a clue about what followed. In the picture, they sit side by side without touching. They aren't even looking at each other. Antonia looks away from the camera, with a very slight smile on her face. Tchaikovsky looks right at the camera. He seems distressed. Maybe he knew what was coming.

The couple left for St. Petersburg so that Tchaikovsky could introduce Antonia to his family. By the time they returned to Moscow a couple of weeks later, he was on the verge of a nervous breakdown. He said that his wife was "physically repulsive." He fled to the country estate of his sister and her husband.

However, he couldn't just run away from his problem. When he returned to Moscow in September, she met him. He had to live with her, and things grew steadily worse. He found that she had lied to him. She didn't know anything about his music. She didn't know any music. In fact, she didn't know much about anything. Many people

A miniature version of the picture taken on Tchaikovsky's wedding day. The bride and groom aren't touching each other, and Tchaikovsky doesn't look very happy.

described her as a very stupid person. Tchaikovsky felt very stifled and confined. One night he almost felt like murdering her. But he didn't. Instead, he tried to murder himself. He waded into the freezing waters of the Moscow River, which ran through the center of the city. He hoped that he would catch pneumonia and die.

He didn't. He ran away again, this time to St. Petersburg. He stayed with his brother Anatol and lay unconscious there for two days. Anatol and a friend went to Antonia and offered her money to go away. To their surprise, she agreed. Under the strict laws of the time, the couple could not get a divorce. Leaving was the best that could be done.

But that was far from the end of things. Later on Antonia went back on her agreement. She continued to bother both Tchaikovsky and his family. Meanwhile she had a series of love affairs with different men. She had children by two of them. And she wrote Tchaikovsky long letters that described these love affairs.

She was eventually declared to be legally insane, but that wasn't until 1896. By then, Tchaikovsky was dead.

In addition to Antonia's personal qualities, there is probably another reason the marriage didn't work out.

Peter Tchaikovsky was a homosexual, and in his era people were much less understanding than they are now. He had to keep his sexual orientation a secret. Perhaps he felt he had to get married so that people wouldn't suspect anything. In fact, the previous year he had written a letter to his brother Modest. "I have decided to get married," he wrote. "It is unavoidable. I must do it." At that time, he didn't have anyone in mind. Maybe Antonia Milyukova simply happened to come around at the right time.

This map gives some idea of the size of Russia, which extends well beyond the right-hand border of the illustration. With an area of 6,592,812 square miles, it is the world's largest country. Canada is a distant second with 3,612,187 square miles. When Russia annexed 15 neighboring countries early in the 1920s to form the Union of Soviet Socialist Republics (USSR), it was even larger. The USSR broke up in 1991.

Sound Recording FYInfo

As the year 1877—so important in Tchaikovsky's life—drew to a close, a momentous event occurred thousands of miles away. In his laboratory in Menlo Park, New Jersey, American inventor Thomas Alva Edison recited the poem "Mary Had a Little Lamb." A few moments later, he and several of his employees listened in amazement as they heard the poem's words come back to them. The sound came not from Edison, but from a small machine placed on a table. Edison had just invented the phonograph.

His original machine had a cylinder that was covered with something like modern aluminum foil, only slightly thicker. A stylus, similar to a needle, would react to the sound vibrations of a person speaking and make grooves in the foil as the cylinder was turned using a hand crank. When the cylinder was hooked up to a speaker and turned again, it would reproduce what had just been recorded.

People were astonished. At first they thought it was a fraud. To convince them, Edison asked respected people such as clergymen to try it out in public demonstrations. It worked every time.

But Edison didn't invent the phonograph to record music. He believed that it would mainly be used in business as a dictating machine. In fact, once he invented the phonograph, he lost interest in it.

Other people, though, were very interested. They made improvements to the original design. A decade later Edison became involved again. Years of intense competition and even more improvements followed. Wax and other materials replaced foil, which quickly wore out or ripped. Then flat disks replaced rotating cylinders. Just before 1900, music began to be recorded. At first, the disks could only hold about two minutes of music. Then someone figured out a way to record on both sides of the disk.

The first big commercial successes were with disks that rotated at a speed of 78 revolutions per minute (rpm). These could hold about five minutes of music on each side. Long-playing records (LPs) were introduced in 1948. They were twelve inches in diameter and the standard speed was 33^1/3 rpm. Many played an entire symphony on one side and a second symphony on the other.

Then in 1982 compact discs (CDs) were introduced. They were much smaller than LPs but held more music. They are etched and read using lasers, which is much more precise than the old technology.

MP3 players came along in 1997. With this music compression technology, music could be downloaded from the Internet for free and put onto a computer chip. Within a few years, MP3 players could hold the contents of up to fifty CDs. Yet an MP3 player is not much larger than a deck of cards.

In just over a century, technological advances went from a device that could play a very small portion of *Swan Lake* to one that could hold all the music that Tchaikovsky ever wrote.

This is a picture of Tchaikovsky's burial site in the Nevsky Monastery in St. Petersburg. It is a popular tourist destination. Nearby are the graves of composer Nikolay Rimsky-Korsakov and author Fyodor Dostoyevsky. Modest Tchaikovsky said that his brother died after drinking impure water. Some people believe that he may have been poisoned or committed suicide to avoid a scandal.

Masters of Music

CHAPTER 5

The Final Years

With the support of his family and of Nadezhda von Meck, Tchaikovsky was able to move beyond his horrible and very ill-advised marriage. He told Madame von Meck all the awful details of what had happened, though he left one thing out of all the letters that he ever wrote to her: He could never tell her about his homosexuality.

That was about the only thing that they never shared. He constantly referred to her as his "beloved friend." Many of the letters also described the music that he was composing, so we have a record of how he was feeling.

We also have a record of what became an increasing series of travels. Tchaikovsky often spent the chilly Russian winters in southern Europe, returning in the spring to enjoy Russia's warm summers.

By late in 1887 Tchaikovsky was famous well beyond the borders of Russia. He began a tour of Europe that featured his music. He felt it was important that he conduct his own music. To overcome his fear of his head falling off, he took some conducting classes.

He suffered a crushing blow in 1890. Nadezhda von Meck wrote him to say that she was breaking off their relationship. She explained that she had serious financial problems and couldn't support him any longer. It hurt Tchaikovsky deeply to think that someone to whom he had poured out his heart and soul for so many years would regard money as the basis of their relationship. Even if she had never given him another ruble, he still would have valued their friendship. Worse, he soon learned that her financial problems had been solved, yet she still refused to write to him. No one knows why this happened.

In the following year, when Tchaikovsky was about to depart for a concert tour to the United States, another blow fell: His beloved sister died.

Tchaikovsky rented this house in the village of Klin, located on the outskirts of Moscow, during the last few years of his life. It was deep in the woods and provided him with a peaceful setting.

The pain was lessened somewhat by his trans-Atlantic trip. He was favorably received and conducted several concerts of his music in major cities on the East Coast.

The year 1893 began well. He had a reunion with his old governess, Fanny Durbach. He traveled to England to receive an honorary doctorate from Cambridge University. And he began working on his Sixth Symphony.

"I am confident in considering it the best and, above all, the 'most genuinely sincere' of all my works," he wrote in a letter to his nephew two months before the premiere in October 1893. "I love it as I have never loved any of my other musical offspring."

Interestingly, the final work that Mozart, Tchaikovsky's musical idol, was working on just before his death was his *Requiem*. A requiem is a special mass that honors someone who has just died. What would become Tchaikovsky's final work also emphasized death. It was different from any other classical symphony up to that point. The final movements of all previous symphonies were in a fast, upbeat tempo called *allegro*. The Sixth Symphony, on the other hand, ends very quietly. The music simply dies away. Its tempo is called *adagio lamentoso,* which means "slowly and sadly." The movement even contains several bars of music from "Repose the Soul," the Russian Orthodox Church burial service.

Within two weeks, Tchaikovsky himself would die and be buried. Thousands of mourners followed his coffin through the streets of St. Petersburg.

For many years, people accepted the story that his brother Modest had told. At that time, an epidemic of cholera—the same disease that had claimed their mother nearly forty years earlier—was sweeping through St. Petersburg. Because its main cause was

Top: Bedchamber where Tchaikovsky frequently stayed with his friend the Grand Duke Constantin Constantinovic. Bottom: Tchaikovsky's funeral drew thousands of mourners.

drinking impure water, people boiled water to kill the cholera germs. But for some reason, Modest said, Peter drank a glass of unboiled water. He came down with cholera and died four days later. More recently, other theories regarding his death have begun to emerge. One is that he was poisoned. Another is that he was threatened with a scandal and committed suicide to avoid it.

In all likelihood, we will never know for sure.

But one thing is certain: Peter Tchaikovsky was one of the greatest composers who ever lived. More than anyone else, he made Russian music popular around the world. That paved the way for later Russian composers such as Sergei Rachmaninov, Alexander Glazunov, Dmitri Shostakovich, and Igor Stravinsky to make their marks on the musical world.

Tchaikovsky relaxes in the garden of his house at Klin. He composed his ballets Sleeping Beauty *and* The Nutcracker *while he was living here. Today the house and grounds are a museum.*

Left: A modern version of Tchaikovsky's ballet Sleeping Beauty, *staged at the Metropolitan Opera House in New York City. Right: A picture taken in 1890 of members of the cast of the original production of* Sleeping Beauty.

And Tchaikovsky's music goes far beyond Russia. Millions of people have seen his great ballets *Swan Lake, The Nutcracker,* and *Sleeping Beauty.* Millions more have attended live performances of his symphonies, concertos, operas, and chamber music. Still more have listened to recordings of his compositions.

Tchaikovsky wrote some of the most deeply personal music ever written. He could reach the heights of supreme happiness and the depths of extreme despair.

"Undoubtedly I should have gone mad but for music," he once wrote. "Music is indeed the most beautiful of all Heaven's gifts to humanity wandering in the darkness. Alone it calms, enlightens our souls. It is not the straw to which the drowning man clings; but a true friend, refuge and comforter, for whose sake life is worth living." ◆

Vladimir LENIN

When Tchaikovsky was enjoying some of his first successes in 1870, Russian political life was in turmoil. Though the peasants, or serfs, had been legally set free nine years earlier, most were still living in poverty. Small groups of revolutionaries were trying to change the government of the czar.

That year marked the birth of Vladimir Ilyich Lenin. More than anyone else, he would be responsible for the downfall of the czar several decades later and the rise of the Communist party which took control of the government.

Lenin began school at the age of nine in his hometown of Simbirsk, a small town on the broad Volga River about 500 miles east of Moscow. He was a bright boy and did very well in his studies. But when he was seventeen, he received a life-changing shock. His older brother was hanged for his part in a plot to assassinate Czar Alexander III. Lenin began participating in student protests and was expelled from the university in which he had just enrolled. Eventually he gained a law degree, but he also read literature written by earlier Russian revolutionaries. He was especially influenced by the writings of Karl Marx, a German intellectual who wrote the *Communist Manifesto*. Marx believed that the workers should control the government. Lenin wanted to form a political party to advance that belief.

In 1895 he traveled to Europe, where he met other Marxists. Soon after his return, he was arrested for illegal activities but was released after a year in solitary confinement. He spent the next twenty years organizing a party called the Bolsheviks. Eventually he became its leader, and it would become known as the Communist party. It advocated the violent overthrow of the government.

It helped that Czar Nicholas II was steadily losing power. The end came in 1917 during World War I, with the Russians losing a series of battles to the Germans. A democratic government briefly replaced the czar, but Lenin led a revolt in November that year that installed his Bolsheviks in power. Soon afterward, the czar and his entire family were murdered.

After winning a civil war that lasted three years, the Russians then took over fifteen republics in central and southern Asia and established the Union of Soviet Socialist Republics (USSR), more commonly known as the Soviet Union, in 1922. Lenin became the ruler.

Lenin suffered several strokes and died in 1924. He was succeeded by Joseph Stalin, who became a ruthless tyrant. He killed everyone who disagreed with him. By the time of his death in 1953, Stalin had killed millions of Russians from all walks of life.

Lenin's body was embalmed and placed in a glass coffin inside the Lenin Mausoleum in Moscow. People would sometimes wait in line for hours to go inside and silently file past the coffin. In 1924 St. Petersburg—which had been called Petrograd after 1914—was renamed Leningrad in Lenin's honor. But when the Soviet Union collapsed in 1991, the city's residents voted to return Leningrad to its original name.

Selected Works

Ballets
The Nutcracker
Sleeping Beauty
Swan Lake

Operas
Queen of Spades
Eugene Onegin
The Maid of Orléans

Symphonies
Symphony #1, "Winter Dreams"
Symphony #2, "The Little Russian"
Symphony #4
Symphony #5
Symphony #6, "Pathetique"

Concertos
Piano Concerto #1
Piano Concerto #2
Violin Concerto

Other Works
Romeo and Juliet: Fantasy Overture
1812 Overture
Capriccio Italien
Francesca da Rimini

Chronology

1840	Peter Ilyich Tchaikovsky born on May 7
1844	Fanny Durbach becomes family governess
1848	Family moves to Moscow and then to Alapayevsk, near Ural Mountains
1850	Begins studies at School of Jurisprudence in St. Petersburg
1854	Mother dies
1859	Finishes law school and begins working at Ministry of Justice
1863	Leaves job at Ministry of Justice to begin full-time studies at St. Petersburg Conservatory
1866	Leaves St. Petersburg and joins new Moscow Conservatory as teacher
1868	Meets singer Desirée Artot and falls in love, but she marries another man
1869	First opera, *The Voyevoda,* premieres at Bolshoi Theatre in Moscow
1876	Completes *Swan Lake;* meets Leo Tolstoy
1877	Begins association with Madame Nadezhda von Meck, whose support allows him to abandon teaching and work on composing; marries former student Antonia Milyukova, but it soon ends and he attempts to commit suicide
1879	Premiere of opera *Eugene Onegin*
1880	Father dies; writes *1812 Overture*
1887	Begins concert tour of Europe
1890	Relationship with Madame von Meck ends, causing deep depression
1891	Sister dies; begins concert tour of U.S.
1892	*Nutcracker* ballet premieres
1893	Dies on November 6

Timeline in History

1812	Napoléon invades Russia
1827	Ludwig van Beethoven dies
1836	Siege of the Alamo in Texas
1837	Queen Victoria of England begins sixty-four-year reign
1846	Mexican-American war begins; ends two years later as Arizona, California, Nevada, New Mexico, Texas, Utah, and parts of Colorado and Wyoming are added to United States
1848	Karl Marx and Friedrich Engels write *Communist Manifesto*
1854	Crimean War begins
1857	U.S. engineer E. G. Otis installs first safety elevator
1861	U.S. Civil War begins
1862	Civil War battle of ironclad ships *Monitor* and *Merrimac*
1865	Abraham Lincoln assassinated; Civil War ends
1866	Alfred Nobel invents dynamite
1868	First professional baseball team, Cincinnati Red Stockings, is formed
1869	Princeton and Rutgers play first formal intercollegiate football game
1870	Birth of Vladimir Lenin
1876	Custer's Last Stand; Alexander Graham Bell patents the telephone
1877	Thomas Edison patents the phonograph
1878	Edison patents the electric lightbulb
1879	Birth of Albert Einstein
1883	New York's Brooklyn Bridge opens
1889	Birth of Adolf Hitler
1895	Wilhelm Roentgen discovers X rays
1896	First modern Olympic Games held in Athens, Greece
1903	Wright brothers fly the first plane; Henry Ford establishes the Ford Motor Company

Further Reading

For Young Adults

Clark, Elizabeth. *Tchaikovsky*. New York: Franklin Watts, 1988.

Foil, David. *Tchaikovsky: The Ballet Suites*. New York: Black Dog Music Library and Leventhal Publishers, 1995.

Kalman, Esther. *Tchaikovsky Discovers America*. New York: Scholastic, Inc., 2000.

Tames, Richard L. *Peter Ilyich Tchaikovsky*. New York: Franklin Watts, 1991.

Thompson, Wendy. *Pyotr Ilyich Tchaikovsky*. New York: Viking Books, 1993.

Works Consulted

Brown, David. *Tchaikovsky: The Early Years*. New York: W.W. Norton, 1978.

Brown, David. *Tchaikovsky: The Final Years*. New York: W.W. Norton, 1992.

Garden, Edward. *Tchaikovsky*. London: Dent, 1973.

Gee, John, and Elliott Selby. *The Triumph of Tchaikovsky*. New York: The Vanguard Press, 1960.

Hanson, Lawrence, and Elizabeth Hanson. *Tchaikovsky: The Man Behind the Music*. New York: Dodd, Mead & Company, 1966.

Nice, David. *Compact Companions: Tchaikovsky*. New York, Simon & Schuster, 1995.

Pozansky, Alexander. *Tchaikovsky: The Quest for the Inner Man*. New York: Schirmer Books, 1991.

Schonberg, Harold C. *The Lives of the Great Composers*. New York: W.W. Norton & Company, 1981.

Strutte, Wilson. *Tchaikovsky: His Life and Times*. Neptune City, N.J.: Paganiniana Publications, 1981.

Warrack, John. *Tchaikovsky*. New York: Charles Scribner's Sons, 1973.

To Learn More About Tchaikovsky's Private Life

Tchaikovsky, Peter. *To My Best Friend: Correspondence Between Tchaikovsky and Nadezhda Von Meck, 1876-1878*. Clarendon, 1993.

Internet Addresses

Illustrated Biography:
http://www.classicalarchives.com/tchai.html

National Arts Centre from Canada:
http://www.artsalive.ca/en/mus/infozone/tchaikovsky.cfm

Photos and information about Tchaikovsky's work:
http://www.w3.rz-berlin.mpg.de/cmpl.tchaikovsky.html

Life and Work of Tchaikovsky:
http://www.tchaikovsky.host.sk/

Glossary

andante (on-DON-tay)—a piece of music played at a slow tempo

ballet (bal-LAY)—a dance presented with musical accompaniment that often tells a story without using any words

bumpkin (BUMP-kin)—an awkward person, often with very little learning

chamber music (CHAME-ber MYOO-zik)—musical composition for a few instruments, with each playing a different part

cholera (CALL-er-uh)—a disease of the stomach and intestines that is often acquired by drinking impure water

concerto (kon-CHAIR-toe)—a musical composition for orchestra and a solo instrument, usually written in three parts, or movements

confidant (KAHN-fi-dahnt)—an especially close friend to whom a person tells very personal secrets

conservatory (kun-SIR-vuh-tore-ee)—a school of music

czar (ZAHR)—the ruler of Russia. It is sometimes spelled *tsar*

governess (GUH-vur-ness)—a woman hired to watch over and educate children in their home, and who usually lives in the children's house

opera (AH-prah)—a play set to music, in which most or all of the words are sung

overture (OH-ver-chur)—a short orchestral piece that introduces a longer work, such as an opera or ballet

porcelain (POR-seh-lin)—a type of fragile ceramic material used to make fine dishes and ornaments

requiem (REH-kwee-um)—a Catholic mass for the dead

revolutionaries (rev-oh-LOO-shun-air-ees)—people who try to make sudden major changes in the way that things are done or in the way that they are governed

ruble (ROO-bull)—a unit of Russian money, similar to the U.S. dollar

scarlet fever (SCAR-let FEE-ver)—a contagious disease characterized by high fever and bright red (scarlet) skin

symphony (SIM-foe-nee)—a large-scale musical composition for full orchestra, usually consisting of four parts, or movements